Principles and Success Strategies
——FOR——
Everyday Living

By
Ralph Palmen

Star Song
PUBLISHING GROUP

Nashville, Tennessee

Star Song Publishing Group, a division of
    Jubilee Communications, Inc.
2325 Crestmoor, Nashville, Tennessee 37215.
Printed in the United States of America.

First Printing, October 1991

Library of Congress Cataloging-in-Publication Data

Palmen, Ralph
    Principles and success strategies for everyday living / by Ralph Palmen.—1st ed.
        p.   cm.
    ISBN 1-56233-010-1 : $7.95
    1. Self-actualization (Psychology) 2. Self-actualization (Psychology)—Case studies. 3. Success. I. Title. II. Title: Principles and success strategies for everyday living.
    BF637.S4P34   1991
    158'.1—dc20   91-33160
                                                              CIP

ACKNOWLEDGMENT

One of life's great blessings is when God brings someone into your life at the right time to help you with a special task.

God brought such a person into my life in the form of Mark Cutshall. Mark is a splendid editor and writer as well as a gifted creative thinker. His talents and guidance helped turn an unfinished manuscript into a finished product.

Thank you, Mark, for your help and support. You are an example of the theme of this book.

TABLE OF CONTENTS

PART THREE

People of Everyday Living

Conclusion

P-A-R-T
ONE

PRINCIPLES
for Everyday Living

Why do some people succeed in life while others always seem to struggle? What makes the difference between achievement and failure? Between reaching one's full potential and being satisfied with mediocrity?

Do you ever ask yourself these questions as you look around at your work, your family, your future, your life? Then I'd say you've come to the right book!

My purpose in writing this little volume is to help you discover and reach your full potential in life. I want you to recognize your unique talents and desires, so that you can become all that God meant you to be. I want you to be able to live to your full potential in your work, your family, your friendships, your finances, and your faith.

Living to one's full potential—this is something almost everyone wants but few people ever attain. And the secret isn't some magic formula, and I can't offer you "Ten Easy Steps to Success" or a set of pat answers that solve all of life's problems.

What I can offer you are the ideas of this book, ideas that will so intrigue and excite you that you'll want to *live* them. And you *can* live them because what you find in this book is exactly what the title suggests . . . .

You'll discover *principles:* practical truths for successfully dealing with people and with life regardless of your situation, background, or age. The six principles in the first section form a foundation upon which you can base your entire life.

You'll learn *success strategies:* solid, everyday approaches for making the six principles work in your life. These are ideas I've used in my own life, and they are methods which have helped thousands. Besides, you are probably using one or more of these strategies right now without even realizing it.

Finally, you'll read stories of *real people*—business owners, students, pastors, homemakers, and others who have put the ideas of this book into practice. Some of these men and women are famous; others are not. What they share, however, is a new source of inner strength, a deeper character, and a greater love for life because each has chosen to reach for their full potential.

These men and women will inspire and surprise you. They are people like John Wordsworth who grew up in Minneapolis, Minnesota. Because his father traveled a lot, John was forced to do most of the chores around the house.

One chilly winter day, John was shoveling snow and thinking about the mountain of household jobs he had to do. After several hours of shoveling, John was ready to quit. He trudged back inside the house.

"I'm tired of working all the time," he told his mother. This wise woman listened to her son and then simply said, "John, the only way you get strong is by working *after* you're tired."

John went back outside and shoveled snow for four more hours. Over the next 50 years, John Wordsworth kept working. He never lost sight of the value of hard work. As the owner of a business, he continually found new ways to apply the truth that hard work pays off.

The story of his determination has a happy ending. Today John Wordsworth is one of the most successful commercial floor contractors in the western United States.

A sound principle, applied through a successful strategy, by a person a lot like you and me. John Wordsworth's story of determination and reward is what this book is all about.

Would you like to experience a life filled with new possibilities for reaching your potential? Would you like to become the person God created you to be? Would you like to turn your dead ends into new beginnings? Would you like to turn your shortcomings into strengths and seize the chance to live to your full potential?

Then turn the page. Because the story of how it all can happen is waiting for you . . . .

The Reward of Choosing a Life Goal

What do you want out of life?

I don't know of any question that's more overwhelming—or more exciting—to answer.

The road to successful everyday living starts with knowing where it is you want to go. It starts with knowing your life goal. I learned one of the best ways to choose a life goal from motivational expert Charlie "Tremendous" Jones. Charlie observed that a person can determine his or her goal in life by answering these three questions:

1. Who will I live my life with?
2. What am I going to live my life in?
3. What am I going to live my life for?

Who will I live my life with?

Think about this first question for a moment. Selecting a mate is obviously very important. Often people get bogged down wondering, "Have I made the right choice?" Charlie Jones believes that it's not as important that you make the right choice as it is that you make your choice right. In other words, guaranteed compatibility isn't the issue. Rather, it's learning to become compatible with your life partner.

What am I going to live my life in?

By this Charlie means, "What kind of work do I desire?" The principle hinges not on determining the perfect job but on being able to live with the job you already have. Charlie says, "A lot of people spend an awful lot of time trying to find 'the right job' when what they should be doing is trying to make the job they have right."

What am I going to live my life for?

This is the third question you must ask to determine your life goal. In order for life to have meaning, I'm convinced that an individual must live for a cause that's bigger than himself. Some of the most unhappy and unproductive people I know are simply living to satisfy their own selfish desires. Without exception, the truly fulfilled folks I meet are living for a cause whose scope and purpose goes far beyond the person's own day-to-day existence. Many of these people are living for God.

Few things are more exciting than determining your goal in life. By answering these three questions, you'll be better able to forge a philosophy of life that will help you determine and then reach a life goal.

Don't allow the challenge of establishing a life goal to overwhelm you. Let it move you to dream as you consider your mate, your work, and whatever it is you seek to accomplish in life.

The Joy of Planning Your Future

Have you ever seen a house that was built without a blueprint? I did once, and it was a sight to behold! There wasn't one straight line in the whole structure. In fact, the house looked so wobbly I feared one good gust of wind would blow it over.

If you want a house that's solid and built to last, you hire an architect and invest whatever effort and energy necessary for a quality product. Yet why do so many people who say they want to build a solid life spend so little time planning their future?

One of the most rewarding things you can ever do is to create a blueprint for living. Developing a plan will help you answer some important questions like, "What do I want out of life?" and "What kind of person do I want to become?"

Here are three ways you can begin to draw up your own blueprint for living:

1. *Picture the completed structure.* What do you want your life to look like? What do you see yourself doing a year from now? Five years from now? Jot down at least three things you would like to accomplish during the next twelve months. The more specific you can be, the better.

2. *Take stock of your building materials.* Whether you know it or not, God created you with distinct skills and talents. List at least five of these. How might you use these "materials" to help you reach the three goals you just considered?

3. *Set a timetable.* When would you like to see some of your blueprints take shape? Give yourself a realistic date for completing the goals you listed above. You'll feel a tremendous amount of satisfaction when you look back and see that you've reached your objectives.

Do you want a life that's wobbly or one that's built on a solid foundation? A person who builds his or her life on the teachings of Jesus is choosing a solid foundation (Matt. 7:24-27).

As you think about the foundation of your life, consider the wisdom of this little verse:

> Isn't it strange that princes and kings
>   and clowns that caper in sawdust rings
>   and common folks like you and me
>   are builders for eternity?
>
> To each is given a life to live,
>   a bag of rules and a bunch of tools
>   and each must shape—'ere life has flown—
>   a stumbling block or stepping stone.

The Satisfaction of Putting Others First

The Reverend A.J. Fast and his wife, Ethyl, invested their lives in raising their two sons. They went to Little League baseball games with young son Darcy. They attended music recitals with older son Dallas. Through the years, the Fasts put the needs of these two boys before their own desires. And today they can see the results.

Darcy pitched in the major leagues for both the Chicago Cubs and the San Diego Padres, and Dallas became an outstanding musician. Today, the entire family lives in Centralia, Washington, where Darcy pastors the fastest-growing church in town. Dallas is minister of music there, and A.J. is minister of visitation.

I love this story because it illustrates the principle of service: You will be richly rewarded when you put the needs of others first. Consider what would happen if more people put this truth to work . . . .

Take the school teacher who moans, "If only my students would behave better! Then I would be a better teacher and we'd all have more fun in class." I wonder if my friend has ever thought of giving her students the attention and learning they desire before thinking about her own frustrations. Do you think their behavior would improve if she did that?

Take the business executive who complains, "If my staff

would just produce a little more, then I'd give them some recognition and praise." What would happen if he first gave his people some much-needed encouragement? What do you think would happen to their productivity?

The principle of service works for employees, too—for the worker saying, "If my boss would just give me a raise, I'd work harder." If this person put effort before his paycheck, he might just receive the raise he's been hoping for.

It's hard to explain why the principle of service works. However, it's not too difficult to confirm what happens when you put it into practice. Jesus said it well: "Give, and it will be given to you" (Luke 6:38).

When you put the needs of another first, you'll experience an inner satisfaction that words can't describe.

The Luxury of Living
One Day at a Time

"Have you noticed that most people really aren't there when they're there?"

With this question, sociologist Tony Campolo shares his observation that so many folks these days fail to live in the present. We don't like our circumstances so we either daydream about the past or fantasize about the future. Either way, we fail to see how full and good life can be right now.

Just about every successful person I've ever known has learned to accept his or her circumstances—the good, the bad, and the ugly. How are they able to do this? One of the main reasons is that they're content to live one day at a time. This isn't a chore but a luxury: the only thing you need to concern yourself with is today (Matt. 6:34).

Imagine how you might feel and how you might see the world a little differently if you decided to live just for today. Imagine . . .

1. Just for today, I will not worry about life's problems. Instead, I will tackle the tasks at hand with enthusiasm and vigor.

2. Just for today, I will expect to be happy, keeping in mind Abraham Lincoln's philosophy that "a person is just about as happy as he makes up his mind to be!"

3. Just for today, I will strengthen my mind. I will learn at least one new fact about my world. I will not be a mental loafer.

Instead, I will read something that stretches my mind and makes me see things in a way I never have before.

4. Just for today, I will exercise my soul by doing something nice for someone else. Instead of wondering, "What's in it for me?," I will concentrate on the one who's receiving until their joy becomes my own.

5. Just for today, I will be agreeable, courteous, and thoughtful. I will not be critical of someone else's faults. Instead, I will approach every interaction as a chance to enable people to see the best in themselves.

6. Just for today, I will take a moment to be quiet and consider all the ways God has blessed me. I will ask Him for guidance and direction so that He might mold my life according to His divine will.

7. Just for today, I will not be afraid. I will let God's power flow through me. Instead of running from my tasks, I will face them with determination and courage.

8. Just for today, I will accept my current circumstances, and I won't complain when things don't go my way. Instead, I will look for the silver lining inside every gray cloud that comes my way.

Let me close by encouraging you, just for today, to embrace life and all the wonderful possibilities it holds—the joys you can't put into words as well as the disappointments you can't ignore. Welcome them all and be glad that you're alive.

If I had to name one thing that characterizes successful and fulfilled people, it would be their belief that nothing is impossible.

Don Bennett is one such person. Don lost his legs in a boating accident several years ago. That didn't stop this business executive from hopping over 14,000 feet to the top of Mt. Rainier. He was able to climb to the top of a mountain because he believed it was possible.

Did you know that every great achievement in science, business, art, education, or religion was built on the cornerstone of a central belief? Christopher Columbus discovered the New World because he believed that the earth was round. Henry Ford revolutionized transportation because he believed it was possible to mass-produce automobiles.

Do you want to experience the power of faith? Then first *consider who or what you believe in*. What is your central belief in life? People who choose to believe in God find Him a source of strength and guidance.

Second, *research the object of your faith*. If you want to develop your faith in God's goodness, for instance, get to know God better. Read the Bible; spend time in prayer and worship. Also, learn from other people. You can get to know more about God's goodness through the testimonies of people who know Him.

Third, *reinforce your choice to believe*. Belief is a choice. If you doubt this, ask yourself why you believe the things you do. Answering this question is a good way to gain a better understanding of the beliefs you hold.

One of the most fulfilled people I've ever met is Dr. Robert Schuller. He turned a drive-in movie theatre into the Garden Grove Community Church, known today as The Crystal Cathedral. He also has the most faith of anyone I've ever met.

Dr. Schuller's positive outlook and his faith come from the same source. Like millions of others who know God, Dr. Schuller knows the power of faith: because of God, nothing is impossible.

What seems impossible for you? When you ask yourself that question, consider that the power of faith is only as great as the object of that faith.

Ralph Waldo Emerson, the great American writer/philosopher, once wrote, "Few men find themselves before they die." Socrates, the Greek teacher and philosopher who also knew something about human nature, said, "Know thyself."

You may know what you want out of life. You may have drawn up a blueprint for your life. You may know how to serve others. You may be perfectly content to accept your present circumstances. You may already trust God. But do you really know yourself?

It seems that nearly all men and women are in a constant struggle to know who they are. People spend millions of dollars in psychological tests and counseling sessions to find out, "Why am I here on this earth?" and "What is my purpose in life?" We turn to self-help seminars, astrological charts, and pop psychologists who dispense professional "wisdom" in between commercials for pimple cream and light beer. Our entire society is caught up in The Great Search for Meaning, in the effort to try to find ourselves.

Jesus Christ offered one of the strangest solutions for "finding yourself." He said, "Whoever finds his life will lose it, and whoever loses his life for my sake will find it" (Matt. 10:39).

Do you truly want to find yourself? Then lose yourself in a being who is infinitely larger than you or me. You will then discover that finding yourself is really a matter of serving others.

The most fulfilled men and women I know have "found themselves" in the lives of the people, the noble cause, and the God whom they served.

How did they do it? How were they able to make these six principles real in their everyday lives? You'll find the answer to this question in the next section's **Success Strategies for Everyday Living.**

P·A·R·T

TWO

SUCCESS STRATEGIES
for Everyday Living

I once knew a man who bought a professional leather craft set. This man loved leather and wanted to be able to make beautiful wallets, belts, and vests. For weeks he studied how to do this. He read about the techniques for cutting and stitching together cowhide. He knew all the principles of expert leather crafting.

But two years after my friend bought his leather kit, he had still failed to make even one item. He was fascinated by leather and knew a lot about it, but he never got around to doing anything with his knowledge. Friends and relatives waited for him to use his enthusiasm and skilled hands to transform pieces of leather into beautiful works of art. Instead, the kit collected dust, and my friend's potential went to waste.

I meet a lot of people like this man: they never seem to get around to tapping into their potential. Their unique God-given abilities, their potential, their "leather craft kits" sit unopened on the shelf. They know the principles, but they're not sure how to put them into practice.

Do you know people like this? Are you yourself a person like that? Would you like to live out the principles outlined in the previous section and thus experience a significant and positive change in your life?

The following strategies are meant to help you do just that. Each is a practical "how to" for applying the principles you've just read about. From developing personal integrity to picking yourself up after defeat to learning how to save for a rainy day, the strategies in this section are practices you can use today. They are methods for experiencing the life truths you may already believe but have hesitated to live out.

And how can you know if these strategies really make a difference? Once you've read a few and practiced the suggestions, ask yourself, "Is my leather kit still on the shelf, or have I opened it up and discovered the tools that can help me craft my life into something beautiful and worthwhile? Am I content to simply think about the principles I know, or am I eager to live them out?"

After two years, my friend opened up his leather kit and began to practice his craft. Within five months, he astounded his family by creating pieces that were both functional and attractive. From then on, he didn't just read about leather work—he also did his craft.

This section of the book is filled with valuable tools for tapping into your potential. Once you get your hands on these success strategies, I think you'll know why it's so much more rewarding to live life than to merely leave it on the shelf.

Self-affirmation. It's one of the most popular terms of the last ten years. Seminar leaders, pop psychologists, movie stars, and talk-show hosts trumpet the promise of self-affirmation loud and long. But does self-affirmation work?

I believe it does. And I've discovered that three aspects of self-affirmation are suggested by the following phrases. How you use these three statements can have a tremendous impact on who you are and what you accomplish in life.

"I am" is the first phrase. What kind of person are you? What is your self-concept, your self-worth? List all the things that you feel make up your personality. What are your outstanding talents and unique traits? Write down every positive thing you can think of to complete the sentence, "I am . . .".

"I can" is the second phrase I associate with self-affirmation. What can you do? Once you've taken a look at who you are, picture what you can do in life. What are your special dreams and desires? What challenges you? What would you like to accomplish? Beginning with the phrase "I can," write a sentence to describe each goal you have set for yourself.

"I will" is the third phrase. The word "will" is a sign of commitment. When you say, "I will," you promise yourself to fulfill your stated goal. From your "I can" list, choose the goals you would like to reach during the next year. Review your statements. Then imagine yourself reaching each of these desired goals.

When I was 23, I attended a series of seminars by a well-known public speaker. As I listened to him, I was challenged by the thought that I could do what he was doing. I said to myself, "I would sure enjoy sharing ideas that challenge others. I can develop the skills of a public speaker, and I'll start at once to learn and practice these skills." Thirteen years later, I was making a living as a professional speaker.

I am. I can. I will. If you consistently use these three phrases as I've described here, then you're bound to see yourself in a different light. Affirm who you are. Affirm what you can do. Affirm your will to reach your goals. And you will never be quite the same person you were before.

How to Create Enthusiasm

There are two types of public speakers—those who put you to sleep and those who set you on fire. The first kind makes me wish my chair came equipped with a pillow. The second makes me want to shout. Speakers like that move me to act, and it's all because of the enthusiasm they generate.

Enthusiasm is the fuse that ignites the minds and fires the imagination. Enthusiasm charges the battery of old ideas that have gone dead with time. Enthusiasm is a high-voltage jolt to the will that says, "Let's go! I can't wait to try!" And enthusiasm can power any dream imaginable.

So how do you get enthusiasm? How do you rev up your engine when the gas gauge points to "E"? I'll never forget a speaker named Alan Cimberg. He started out in fourth gear and didn't slow down until he had the audience pleading for more. His presentation was electric. I was captivated—and taking notes—right from the start.

After ten minutes, Cimberg stopped and asked the audience, "Does anybody know what I've just said?" I—and the 200 others—looked at the notes in front of us. One by one we scratched our heads.

Then Cimberg said, "I just wanted to prove to you that when you're enthusiastic, people will listen—even if they don't know what you're talking about!"

I thought to myself, "If this man can excite an audience by rambling on about nothing, imagine the genuine excitement an enthusiastic speaker could generate if he really had something to say." Alan Cimberg showed me that enthusiasm works and how I could make it real in my own life.

Too many people are afraid to show their emotions. They work hard to be "cool" and in control. They fail to see that emotion—specifically enthusiasm—is capable of making a project a success. Enthusiasm creates more productive employees. Enthusiasm helps meet sales goals. And enthusiasm wins ball games.

Frank Bettger was a minor league baseball player in 1907. He was fired by a manager who told him he looked lazy dragging himself around the field. Frank Bettger was demoted to a lower division team, and his monthly salary dropped from $175 to $25.

Bettger decided he wouldn't get fired for the same reason twice, and he began to play with new enthusiasm. He earned the nickname "Pep" Bettger. Within ten days, he was back in the higher league, earning $185. Within two years, he was playing third base for the St. Louis Cardinals. His baseball skills had not improved significantly, but his enthusiasm created new opportunities he had never dreamed possible.

If you want to be more enthusiastic, look for the things in life you believe in most. Allow your excitement to bubble over. Don't hold back. Your enthusiasm will be contagious. And if people choose not to respond, you've lost nothing.

How to Take Risks

I can still remember the scene: My one-year-old son Mark was sitting on a little hassock that stood about two feet off the floor when he decided that he wanted to walk off the hassock.

He stood up on the hassock, took one big step forward, and immediately fell down on the floor. Then he got back up on the hassock and tried to walk. He fell down again.

Mark kept trying to step off the hassock, land on his feet, and keep moving. Finally he did it. I can still see Mark landing on his feet for the first time and squealing with glee.

Mark failed at least 20 times before he made his first successful leap, but he learned to walk off the hassock because he was willing to take a risk. He didn't get discouraged. He just kept trying—and risking—until he made it.

One of the reasons people don't succeed in their work, their relationships, or their lives is that they're afraid to take risks. They're afraid to fail. They're afraid to step off the hassock and try again if they fall.

The next time you're challenged to step out into uncharted territory, weigh your possible gain against the likelihood of failure. I bet you'll see that the chance for success is worth the necessary risk. Look at Mark. He risked a small bump on the head for the chance to accomplish the seemingly impossible task of landing on his feet and walking.

Taking risks is hard. It's also downright scary—but consider the potential gain that awaits you just beyond the hassock.

When I was a very young man, I read a newspaper article about the "Quick Start Concept." It said that "the first hour of every day should be your best." The idea of getting off to a fast start has always impressed me. I like the way speaker Ed Foreman expresses this truth in his "Ten Commandments for Success and Happiness":

1. Thou shalt get up early, eliminating the need to rush into work, frustrated and late.

2. Thou shalt read or listen to something inspirational and uplifting upon waking.

3. Thou shalt get some exercise each morning to stimulate your heart, lungs, and mind.

4. Thou shalt have some breakfast to keep thyself from being cranky.

5. Thou shalt package thyself appropriately and attractively to feel good about thyself and to be comfortable meeting others during the day.

6. Thou shalt always greet others positively, enthusiastically, and with a smile.

7. Thou shalt always say "terrific" when asked how you are.

8. Thou shalt always be cheerful when conversing with

others. Discuss positive, uplifting thoughts about clients and your business.

9. Thou shalt organize thy tasks and stay at them systematically. Do what needs to be done—when it needs to be done. If you get behind, ask for help. If you get caught up, help others.

10. Thou shalt be treated as you treat others. Be kind and supportive, and you'll find others supporting you.

You will enjoy a more productive and abundant life if you apply these principles in your daily activities. When you start well, you finish well. Why not concentrate on practicing one commandment per month? A year from now you will like yourself a whole lot better!

How to Concentrate

As a lover of sports, I'm always amazed when a favored team gets beaten by an underdog, and it happens all the time. The top team with its overwhelming load of talent and superior coaching gets upended by a weaker squad. How can "losers" come out on top?

I believe the reason is concentration. Concentration is the "hidden player" which favored teams sometimes fail to suit up. Members on the superior team are already thinking about next week's contest, and they fail to concentrate on the current game. The underdog players, however, give their full attention to the contest at hand. The result? The "weaker" team plays a better game and wins. Final score? Concentration, 79; Overconfidence, 0.

The same kind of concentration that causes teams to win games can make you victorious in life. By learning to concentrate on a single task, you'll be able to give yourself totally to whatever it is you're involved in.

The next time you read a book, listen to a friend, or play a sport, give your full attention to that one act. It may not be easy, but by concentrating you'll experience the unmistakable satisfaction of immersing yourself in the task at hand. And you'll also discover a built-in benefit: the more you practice concentrating, the easier it becomes.

Did your mind wander as you read the previous page? If so, let your thoughts wander back to this present moment. Remember that concentration is too valuable to lose. It can help you focus on circumstances, people, and events that might otherwise defeat you.

Concentration. It can sharpen your mind and point you in a winning direction.

Integrity. It's one of the most important qualities you can possess. I don't know anyone who's reached his or her goal in life without valuing integrity.

What is integrity and to what degree is it real in your life? The following story may help you answer both questions.

On his first day of work, a new prison warden decided to interview the inmates. He asked each of them these questions: "What crime were you convicted of?" and "Are you guilty?"

One by one, the prisoners come into the warden's office and explained why they were behind bars. And one by one each told the warden, "No, I'm not guilty. In fact, I was a victim of circumstance."

Each prisoner put the blame on someone else—except one inmate who looked at the warden and said, "Well, yes, I am guilty." The warden replied, "I'm going to have to let you go because I can't have a guilty prisoner in here corrupting all these innocent ones!"

This prisoner was "guilty" of a high degree of integrity—at least at this point in his life! Whatever the reason he was in prison, now he told the truth. Now he was honest with himself and the warden, and he was willing to take responsibility for his actions. Now this prisoner had a code of ethics he was willing to live by.

Like the prisoner, you and I face situations every day that build and test our integrity. When you face a tough challenge, do you slough it off or do you tackle it head on? When the supermarket check-out clerk gives you too much change, do you keep it or point out the error? At home when you sweep the floor, do you use the dustpan to get the last little pile of dirt, or do you sweep it under the rug?

Integrity is built at the work desk, in the check-out line, and in the little corners of life. If you can be honest and faithful to the truth in these small situations, you'll be practicing the kind of personal integrity that will shine during life's more difficult tests.

Have you ever read the life story of a famous person and discovered that the reason he was so accomplished was that he stayed in bed until noon and dilly-dallied the day away?

Success and poor time management. The two never go together. One of the most significant things you can do to improve your productivity and competitive edge is knowing how to make the most of your time. Here are four specific ways you can stretch the hours of the day to meet your goals for that day:

1. *Rise early.* What is one thing that top executives and political leaders have in common? They get up early. They start to work while others are still rubbing their eyes. If you were to get up a half hour earlier than you do now, then in the course of a year you would add 182 more hours—or more than seven days—to your life.

2. *Get off to a positive start.* Think about the time it takes you to get ready, and then allow a little extra time to study, read a good book, or listen to an uplifting cassette tape. When you put good ideas in your head at the start of the day, you'll see the world in a brighter light.

3. *Keep a monthly calendar.* Having a written plan will give you a sense of direction and purpose for the day. Note your meetings, appointments, and deadlines, and you'll learn to appreciate time as a precious commodity to be used wisely.

4. *Determine your daily priorities.* Ask yourself, "What's the most important thing I need to do today?" Then schedule the day's tasks in descending order of importance. Start the day by working on your Number One task. When it's complete, go on to your next task. You'll enjoy a sense of fulfillment as you finish each job.

Time. A lot of people fret that there never seems to be enough of it. Yet those who know how to make the most of their hours aren't complaining. They're too busy reaching their goals! And because they're usually exhausted from putting in a good day's work, they enjoy the added reward of wise time management—a good night's sleep.

How to Get More "Smileage"

Question: What's an extremely valuable resource that can enrich your life but costs nothing to own or to share? Clue: It's a personal possession. Though it's something you'd never want to lose, the more you give it away, the easier it is to own.

This valuable resource is your smile. Do you take it for granted? Consider what a smile can mean to someone else! Research has shown that salespeople who smile at their customers close more deals. Doctors who smile at their patients have fewer malpractice suits than physicians who are more somber. Besides, it takes fewer muscles to smile than frown!

Of all the people you know, whose smile comes immediately to mind? How do you feel when you're around this person? What qualities does he or she bring out in you that you enjoy? Do you walk away smiling?

If the corners of your mouth just turned up, then the benefits of a smile don't have to be put into words. They're already written across your face!

How important is it to smile? Willy Sutton, the famous bank robber, once said, "You can get more with a smile and a gun than you can with just a smile." What he meant was that you need more than a smile to "get the job done." A smile won't take the place of integrity, honesty, ability, and a true desire to serve others. A smile can, however, help build a bridge between you and another person. A smile says, "Come. Let's walk together."

Whether it's seen by a stranger or a friend, your smile is a greeting that speaks louder then words. It's a spontaneous sign of welcome, a calling card to the heart. Your smile is an invitation to friendship for all to see and reflect.

How to Deal with Change

Someone once said that the only unchanging thing in life is change itself. And how you respond to change—how well you're able to react to a new set of circumstances—can mean the difference between success and failure in almost any area of life. Since change is here to stay, the issue to deal with is how to cope with change.

The people of Switzerland know about change and the action it demands. For years, Swiss watches were Number One in the world. Then, in the early 1970s, the Japanese flooded the market with inexpensive quartz watches. In 1974, the Swiss share of the world market plunged from 30 percent to a mere 9 percent.

How did this one-time world leader respond to change? The Swiss developed a new timepiece called The Swatch, a waterproof watch with a band made of tough, colorful plastic. Surveys now reveal that the average consumer owns three Swatches, and the Swiss are back on top of the watch world.

The Swiss had to act quickly and wisely, though. Their survival in the marketplace depended on making a decision that was swift and smart. They reviewed all the facts about their competitors, the buying public, and their own product—and then they acted.

When faced with change, you can either procrastinate until

it's too late, or you can act on the best available evidence. As a rule, the more decisive you are, the better chance you have of beating the culprit called time that constantly works to reduce your opportunities for success.

Where do you need to be decisive in dealing with change? Consider these "action steps." First, brainstorm your best options for action. Next, estimate the amount of time you can reasonably take before indecisiveness becomes your enemy. Then, be like the Swiss and go for it!

"I love my work—it's the *people* I have a hard time with!"

Sooner or later it's bound to happen. In a business meeting. On a family vacation. At school. Or at home. At some point, you're going to experience "people problems."

Perhaps it will be a personal disagreement, a personality conflict, or a misunderstanding. "People problems" are a fact of life, and how you handle them can make a significant impact on your success. Basically, you have three options for dealing with "people problems."

First, you could try to *change the situation*. You know the thoughts: "If I could just escape this environment—run away from home, quit the job, dump my spouse, drop out of school, and get away from the situation—then my problem would be solved."

I knew a man who got physically sick whenever he felt the pressure to produce at work. His physical stress gave him a good reason to quit or be fired. Running away from the job, however, didn't help him. And running away from your problem won't work for you. Changing the situation doesn't solve problems. In fact, the runaway quickly finds that the very same "people problems" exist in the new environment.

Second, you could try to *change the person* with whom you're having problems. Does this sound familiar? "If only I could get her to change the way she acts towards me" or "if I could just get him to shape up and do things the way he should, then I wouldn't have so many problems." Trying to change another person is frustrating and fruitless. No matter how hard you try, you can be assured that the other person won't meet your expectations.

By changing *yourself,* however, you have the greatest opportunity for making a positive impact both in your own life and that of someone else. The next time you fail to "click" with another person, ask yourself, "How can I improve our relationship? How can I do things differently?"

Be willing to sacrifice. Take positive control of your thoughts and actions. If you change yourself rather than trying to change the situation or the other person, you may find the rest of the world reflecting that change in a positive way.

How to Say "I'm Sorry"

"I'm sorry." Those are two of the most difficult and important words you'll ever say. Let me tell you a little story that illustrates what I mean.

One Monday morning I arrived at my office and found Sunday's newspaper scattered all over the parking lot. As I looked at the slot in the front door for the paper and mail, I wondered, "Now why didn't the paper get dropped inside?" I called the newspaper office and complained that Sunday's edition had been blown into the next county and that I'd like a new paper.

The next evening, a young boy trooped into my office. His cheeks were red from the sting of the cold air. His eyes sparkled as he said, "I'm your new paperboy and I'm sorry about your newspaper. I left it outside because I was afraid it would scatter all over your floor if I put it through the slot. I'll do better in the future."

I was really touched by this boy's honesty. I was impressed by his willingness to assume responsibility for his actions and decided that he'd be tipped well the next time he came to collect.

This boy also showed me why it's important to take responsibility for your actions. The natural human tendency is to look for someone to blame. When you face up to your mistakes and tell someone that you're sorry, though, two things happen. First, you accept yourself and see the areas where you need to grow.

Second, you give the other person an opportunity to forgive you. The result is that, in forgiving and moving on, your relationship becomes stronger than before.

I discovered each of these rewards because a young boy was willing to say two of the hardest words in the English language.

When was the last time you said, "I'm sorry"? The sound of these two words may be hard on your ears, but they're soft on the heart of the one to whom you're speaking.

Imagine owning a store. Doesn't it seem logical that the longer you kept your doors open, the more customers you'd bring in? Sometimes it pays to put logic on the shelf and be innovative.

A Dallas, Texas, company called Tuesday Morning, Inc. has shown its innovation by shutting its doors. A discount store, Tuesday Morning buys close-out merchandise. These "seconds" aren't particularly unusual, but the way they're sold is.

The company's 56 stores are open only five months out of the year. Research has shown that March, June, September, November, and December are the peak seasonal buying months, so Tuesday's puts out the "open" sign during these times only. They use the remaining months to stock and reorder.

This illogical and innovative approach results in a huge sales volume in a short period of time. It also means a lower overhead and higher profits.

Tuesday Morning shows that it pays to be different. The owners have practiced these three key principles of successful innovation:

Creativity—the ability to see past old, tired habits and imagine new possibilities.

Courage—the boldness to risk in order to reach new heights.

Planning—the foresight to organize every available resource for its greatest possible use.

Somewhere in your life right now, there's a chance for you to be innovative and wonderfully illogical. Take the step! Be creative. Be bold. Be ready to act. And be forewarned—your solution may stand reason on its head and turn your life upside down in the best possible way.

How to Lose the Blues

Can you think of a time when you felt so down you didn't know what to do? I can.

Years ago when I was a salesman, there was a time when business was very slow. I had spent the night in Portland, Oregon. When I woke up in the morning, I discovered that someone had broken a window in my car and stolen all of my clothes. I looked in the backseat and realized that all of my worldly goods were gone. I was low.

Mild depression can take the form of a brief emotional letdown, a lack of confidence, or a bout with apathy. What can you do during these times when life seems to move in slow-motion and you get far fewer things done in a given amount of time? What can you do to move on from the "I don't care" mode?

Dr. Richard Parrott, a successful pastor and counselor, suggests four ways to deal with the blues:

1. *Open up.* When you're feeling down, talk to people. Discuss your feelings with someone you trust. You might want to talk to a professional counselor. Talking about your situation will help you better understand your feelings and help you build relationships with people who care for you.

2. *Get involved.* Take part in activities with other people. Feeling down is often a result of being too "I"-centered or of simply being selfish. As you begin to think about others and reach

out to help make their lives a little better, you'll focus less on your own problems and be less likely to feel down.

3. *Do something.* One of the best ways to beat the blues is to pick a task and do it. Clean the garage. Mow the lawn. Paint a picture. Run, jog, or walk. When you lose yourself in a physical activity, you'll find yourself thinking more about accomplishing the task at hand and less about the blues.

4. *Meet those who inspire you.* Finally, Dr. Parrott suggests that a good way to lose the blues is to get to know some inspirational people. These can be either personal friends or people you meet in a book. When you rub shoulders with great people and their great ideas, a little bit of their enthusiasm for life is bound to rub off on you.

Losing the blues means finding a new desire for living. It can mean the end of a frustrating passage and the beginning of a new path in life.

What's wrong with the following statement? "I've lost my fortune by making some unwise investments. It's too late to start over. My family and I will live out our lives in disgrace and poverty."

Answer: The statement is only partly true. The man who confessed this to me was guilty of making decisions based on opinions rather than facts. The only real fact was that he had lost his fortune through unwise investments. Everything else was strictly opinion. By not basing his outlook on fact, this man missed a truth that stares people in the face every day: *It's never too late to start over.*

Do you feel like giving up on some part of your life right now? Don't. History is full of people who made unwise decisions, lost great fortunes, and rebuilt their lives.

William Danforth, founder of the Ralston Purina Company, lost his entire fortune in the stock market crash of 1929. He regrouped, however, and built one of America's most successful manufacturing companies.

William Danforth and others like him base their comebacks on facts, not opinions. Each acts on the best available evidence to arrive at success. The next time you wonder if you're basing a decision on the facts at hand, ask yourself these questions:

- Have I turned to all of my available resources—people, books, God?
- Have I given myself a reasonable period of time to weigh the pros and cons of my choice?
- Am I willing to make my decision on the basis of the facts at hand and not my emotions?

Wise decisions don't just happen. If you want to preserve a positive outlook, make sure your decisions are based on fact, not fiction. Then, whether you're on a mountaintop, tumbling down a cliff, or just picking yourself up from a fall, you'll be able to dust yourself off and start over.

How to Make Persistence Pay Off

I once met a salesman who had just returned from closing a deal. "How long did your meeting take?" I asked him.

"Two years!" he replied.

At first I was shocked by the answer. Then I found out why he was beaming. He had been calling on the same prospect for more than two years. Finally, after months of phone calls and friendly follow-ups, the client had said, "Yes."

This salesman didn't possess world-class charm or striking good looks. What he did have was that one characteristic all great salespeople have: he had persistence, that undaunted desire to keep trying.

Mark Twain once said, "If a cat sits on a hot stove, it will never sit on a hot stove again. But then it won't sit on a cold stove either. It just gets out of the business of sitting on stoves."

Without persistence, you and I are just like that cat. We try something and if it doesn't turn out quite the way we expected—if we get burned—then we're tempted to give up. We get out of the business of trying.

Marilyn Kourilsky, a professor of economics at the University of California, has concluded that persistence is the most consistent quality of successful entrepreneurs—and, I would add, in people who reach their full potential. She notes that persistence is easy to see in children. We've all seen children so caught up in the excitement of trying their stunts again and again that giving up is not even an option.

In what areas are you tempted to give up? You can benefit in the long run by practicing some joyful, childlike persistence. Like a kid, my salesman friend threw himself into his profession. By being persistent, he turned his profession into play. For him—and for you—persistence costs a lot in terms of effort, but the personal payoff can be tremendous.

Sometimes when my daughter Cheryl complains that things aren't going well in life, I'll look at her with a faint smile and say, "Don't worry. Things are bound to get worse." Usually this causes her to laugh. Deep down, she knows that life isn't bound to get worse, but better.

Cheryl knows what it means to have hope, that precious commodity that has been defined as "an expectation that something we desire is going to happen in the future."

So many people I meet want to have hope, but they don't know how—especially when they've developed the habit of expecting the worst out of life. I could tell them that hard times actually produce hope. Instead I tell them the following story.

I once met a businessman who came close to the edge of financial ruin. He confessed to me, "You know, Ralph, as hard as it's been, I wouldn't trade the past two years for anything. I've learned more about controlling costs, being productive with my time, and getting my employees to produce than any success could have taught me. In fact, I'm looking forward to some outstanding business times in the days ahead."

This man was hopeful because he was able to see his near-failure as a learning experience instead of as a dead end. As a result, he now looks ahead to a brighter future. He's learned that the seeds of hope are often planted in life's rockiest soil. If you approach your task with patience and hard work, you'll see hope bloom in ways you never imagined.

Do you know where to find hope? Just look at a difficult situation that recently was resolved in your own life. The positive outcome you experienced is proof—even when hope seems buried in the worst situations—that good things are possible.

How to Make Good
on Your Commitments

"I'm looking for someone who will follow through." You've heard those words before—from a teacher, parent, boss, or coach. Whether they referred to a reading assignment, a household chore, an important project, or a big game, what the other person wanted to know was, "How important is this to you? Can you commit yourself to the task?"

Commitment. We admire it so much in others because we realize how costly it is in our own life. Early in my career I accepted the challenge of building an executive recruiting division for my employer, a very difficult assignment. Often I had to work late, far beyond the 40 hours for which I was getting paid, and that meant I missed out on a lot of things. However, the strength and discipline I developed have since produced many tangible benefits in my life.

If you think the cost of commitment is too high, then think about the people who have already invested in you:

Commitment is what leads your pastor to visit you when you're in the hospital.

Commitment is what makes your teacher stay after class to help you figure out a math problem.

Commitment is what moves your wife to iron your shirts at 10:30 p.m. when she is so tired she can barely stand up.

Commitment is what makes your husband paint the house when he'd rather be fishing.

Commitment means giving when you don't have to and sacrificing when you don't want to. When I worked all those extra hours, I didn't feel all that wonderful, but reaching my goal made the sacrifices worthwhile.

Where are you making your biggest investment of time, energy, and/or money right now? If your sacrifice is from the heart, then you can't help but become a changed person. Commitment has a way of doing that.

Think of the person you most admire in life. It might be a teacher, a close friend, or a parent. Do you find yourself wondering things like, "How does she do it? How does she get up every morning at 6:00 and run three miles before work?" Or "How does he find the time to read more books in one month than I do in an entire year?" Or "How does she stay so thin?"

In each case, your Most Admirable Person has probably developed a set of good habits. It's a fact that successful people become fit, well read, and well nourished because they develop good habits.

Would you like to develop habits that will help you achieve your desired goals? You can because the practice of developing good habits begins with you.

Habits aren't tendencies you automatically have at birth. They aren't skills you develop at random. Habits are patterns you acquire. They come with repetition and practice until the desired thought or action becomes second nature.

Chris Evert can hit a perfect backhand because she has slammed thousands of them before. James Michener can create a stirring book because he's developed the habit of writing every day.

Habits are just as real for common folk. I recently moved my wastebasket from the left to the right side of my desk. Immediately after the switch, I was amazed at how often I threw paper on the floor—out of habit.

Would you like to develop a new habit or perhaps exchange a bad habit for a good one? First, pick an everyday habit you'd like to change. Personally, I'm trying to eat less. I also want to develop a daily exercise program.

Second, give yourself a reasonable amount of time to make the change. In his book *Psycho-cybernetics,* Dr. Maxwell Maltz states that it takes at least 21 days of conscious effort to establish a new habit.

Third, expect that your new habit will have a positive and permanent impact on your life. A friend of mine went through a rough period with his company before he made a tremendous breakthrough. I asked him, "Stu, how did you remain so 'up' throughout the whole ordeal?"

He said, "I got into the habit of reading the Bible for 15 minutes every morning and every night. I prayed and meditated and emptied all thoughts of discouragement from my mind. By repeating this procedure faithfully every day, I came through the storm with flying colors."

Good habits are no more difficult to establish than bad ones. The question is, "Which kind of habits will you create for yourself?" And what are you waiting for?

How to Develop High Self-Esteem

What gives a person high self-esteem? For years I've believed that a person's self-image is closely tied to the ability to achieve his or her potential. My hunch was supported by George Gallup, Jr. who conducted a poll on self-esteem in America. Gallup found that people with a high degree of self-esteem tend to be high achievers. He also discovered that productive men and women share eight characteristics:

1. *High Morals*—Each of the individuals polled had a high moral and ethical sensitivity.
2. *Family Ties*—Each person felt a strong tie to his or her family, and each believed in traditional family roles.
3. *Relationships*—The people were more successful in their relationships than those with lower self-esteem.
4. *View of Success*—Their understanding of success was rooted in relationships with people rather than in materialism.
5. *Productivity*—People with high self-esteem got more done on their jobs and felt better about their work than those whose self-esteem was lower.
6. *Abstinence*—People with high self-esteem had a far lower incidence of chemical addiction and tended to avoid drugs and alcohol.
7. *Social Involvement*—Each person was more likely to

work for the good of the community and get involved in social and/or political activities.

8. *Generosity*—Each person gave generously of their time and money to help people, causes, and churches.

Not every person with high self-esteem has all these traits. But the point is clear. If you feel good about yourself, you'll tend to feel good about your life, your family, and your work. See if you can identify in yourself at least three of the characteristics listed above. Look for these same qualities in others, and let them be a mirror for you. Then, when you recognize their successes, you'll strengthen your own sense of self-esteem.

How to Create a Larger Fishbowl

The next time I visit the Seattle Aquarium I'm going to look at the goldfish. Why? Because of something a pet store owner once told me. "If you move a fish from a small tank to a big one," he explained, "the fish will begin to grow. Somehow the larger bowl is a signal to the fish to start growing. Small tanks produce small fish and big tanks produce big fish."

Whenever I wonder if I'm growing in a particular area of my life, I take a look at the size of my fish tank. Challenges that at first seem to swallow me up actually give me the needed room to move and grow. Small fish tanks with their tired routine and lack of challenge not only stunt my growth, but they cause me to shrink.

If you really want to grow in life, you need to know how to expand the size of your fish tank. One way to do this is to encourage others. Well-deserved praise enlarges a person's self-respect. Praise breeds confidence in another and inspires him or her to seek bigger arenas filled with new and bigger opportunities. Undue criticism does just the opposite. Critical, hostile words merely stifle people's enthusiasm and cause them to retreat to the small corners of life.

Good training is another excellent way to enlarge the size of your fish tank. People who have been well-trained possess a certain poise in their work. They strive for quality and make fewer errors. On the other hand, a person who has not received good training often repeats the same mistakes and thus fails to grow.

How big is your fish tank at work, at home, at church? Are small challenges inhibiting your growth? Or is your present setting large enough for you to expand your vision? Are you prepared to change tanks if you see that you need a larger pond?

You might also check to see who else is swimming in your tank. Like you, they may have plans to find a bigger bowl. That's good because together you may find it easier to enlarge your fish tank—and you just might encourage a few minnows who are looking for a new way to grow.

"Are you a hard worker?" Years ago when I worked in an employment agency, I asked that question to every person who came in looking for a job.

Without exception, every applicant said, "Yes, I'm a hard worker." No one ever said, "I'm pretty lazy on the job. I actually don't like work at all." This confused me. Could everyone I met really be such a hard worker?

I discovered a strange pattern: The people who claimed to work hard often proved to be rather unproductive. In contrast, workers who didn't feel the effort of "hard" work were often doing their job effectively and enjoying it in the process. By simply enjoying their jobs, they were working well without feeling the strain. These workers helped me discover that hard work and enjoyment on the job go hand-in-hand.

The luckiest person on the face of the earth is the one who learns to fall in love with work because he or she has stopped slaving away and started living.

I once met an insurance agent who wanted to quit his business because he found it hard to set appointments with potential customers. His records showed that he was an excellent salesman. He set appointments with 90 percent of his contacts and closed sales in most of his presentations.

I saw that my friend's life and income might be totally transformed if he learned to enjoy himself. I suggested he set specific sales goals and reward himself with weekly bonuses. The results? My friend learned how to work hard—and have fun—at the same time.

The next time your job seems harder than it should, ask yourself, "Am I having fun? Do I enjoy what I'm doing?" If your answer is "No," then ask yourself, "How hard have I been working?" Assuming you are matched to the right job, the more you put into your work, the more you will enjoy what you do.

Lack of fulfillment is often the sign of half-hearted effort. And one way to enjoy your work more is to set a few specific daily goals. As you focus on meeting each of them, you'll become more concerned with the task at hand and less caught up with any shortcomings of your job.

Hard work isn't a guarantee that you'll always enjoy what you do. By giving your best effort and rewarding yourself, though, you're bound to be more productive and pleased with your work.

How to Get a Promotion

Would you like a better job? Would you like that opportunity to put your talents to work? Then now is the time to start preparing.

When thinking about your job future, you have a choice to make. You can say to yourself, "Once I get the job, then I'll work hard." I know people who have taken this course. Usually, when the new job comes along, they have been unprepared and ill-equipped to handle their new responsibilities.

The alternative is to prepare yourself for the new job before you get it. You can do this by learning as much as possible about the position you expect to fill. Go to seminars. Read. Support the people for whom you work. Learn what problems your superiors face and help them find solutions. You'll not only increase your knowledge, but you'll literally work yourself into a new job.

And to remind yourself why it's important to plan for a new job, read the following poem by Jess Kenner.

> There's going to be a vacancy
> above you later on.
> Someday you'll find the foreman
> or superintendent gone.

And are you growing big enough
　　when this shall be the case,
To quit the post you're holding now
　　and step into his place?

You do the work you have to do
　　with ease from day to day,
But are you getting ready to
　　deserve the larger pay?
If there should come a vacancy
　　with bigger tasks to do,
Could you step in and fill the place
　　if it were offered you?

Tomorrow's not so far away;
　　nor is the goal you seek.
Today you should be training
　　for the work you'll do next week.
The bigger job is just ahead;
　　each new day changes brings.
Suppose the post were vacant now—
　　could you take care of things?

It's not enough to know enough
　　to hold your place today.
It's not enough to do enough
　　to earn your weekly pay.
Someday there'll be a vacancy
　　with greater tasks to do.
Will you be ready for the place
　　when it shall fall to you?

How to Out-Perform a Machine

One of the biggest trends in manufacturing today is replacing people with robots. Compared to their human counterparts, robots tend to be faster and more accurate. And they don't call in sick.

Machines may be grabbing up more and more jobs. But there's one thing they haven't been programmed to do yet, and that's offer the personal touch of a human being.

How much do people really care about getting "the personal touch"? One place to find out is New York City. If you want to get your car washed in the Big Apple, for $5.00 you can roll it through a machine of sponges and hot suds. Or you can take it to Steve's Detailing for a "Super Cleaning."

What does Steve do that a machine can't? First, he hand washes and towel dries your car. Then he hand rubs and polishes the car with quality wax. Steve and his staff use a toothbrush and cotton swabs to clean every crack and crevice of your car. Every speck of grease under the hood is blasted out with an arc spray. Then Steve hand rubs every inch of upholstery with the finest preservative.

Even though the cost of this detailing service is $145, Steve is averaging two to three customers a day. His steep growth curve is proof that people still care about quality and that they're willing to pay for it.

Steve's service demonstrates something else, too. Until someone can train a robot to pick the lint off a floor mat, human beings are still the best at giving a truly personal and professional touch to a job. A robot may be able to tighten twice as many bolts per hour as a factory worker, but only a human being has the sensitivity to know what pleases another human being.

If you want to really shine on the job, then look for the details a machine can't possibly touch. The tiniest cracks and crevices hold the greatest opportunity for you to provide the personal touch.

Only a person with dedication and skill can reach down and do the job that quality demands. If you strive hard and long enough, people will give you the ultimate compliment: "Look at the job he does! Why, he's a machine!" Now *that* kind of comment could make more than one robot jealous.

Do you like what you do for a living? The more I talk to people about their jobs, the more I'm convinced that success is a by-product of enjoying your work.

People who like their work discover five truths. How many of these principles do you find in your own life?

1. *Accept your work.* Work is a basic fact of life. If you want to eat and wear nice clothes and have a roof over your head, you need to work. Almost everything in life—including a well-earned vacation—demands that you work.

Furthermore, God gave work to us (Gen. 1:28-30). Having created us in His image, God provided the opportunity for us to be as creative and productive as He is. We can be encouraged that we are doing what God created us to do when we create and produce—and are His salt and light in the process.

2. *Value your work.* There are no unimportant jobs in this world. Whether you're in accounting or nursing, whether you're changing tires at a gas station or diapers at home, your work has value. Why not do the best possible job?

3. *Work for yourself.* Believe it or not, you'll always be self-employed. Just because someone else signs your paycheck doesn't mean that you're working for someone else. I once asked a retail merchant, "What's made you so successful?" He replied,

"No matter where I've worked, I've always pretended that I own the place." When you own your work, you can't help but enjoy the job.

Let me also remind you that you and I work for God. He who designed us to work is our boss, and we are to "do everything as unto the Lord" (Col. 3:17).

4. *Improve your work.* Every job can be made better, and the most qualified person to suggest and implement changes is you. Look for ways you can be more productive. The better you get, the more fulfilled you'll be—and it can mean working yourself into a new job.

5. *Relish your work.* As you read this, millions of people are out of work. Thousands more who are employed would gladly trade places with you. Work is a privilege. Relish the chance to invest yourself in a job and thank God for the opportunity to work.

Enjoying your job. It's a matter of having the right perspective and the right attitude—and putting that attitude to work.

How to Conduct a Regular Checkup

Cavett Robert tells the story of a little boy who walked into a drugstore and asked the pharmacist if he could use the telephone. "Go right ahead," replied the man behind the counter.

Shortly into his phone conversation, the little boy asked, "Are you looking for a gardener? . . . Well, then, are you happy with your gardener?"

Again the boy asked, "Do you like his work? Are you satisfied with the job he's doing?" Then he thanked the person he was talking to, hung up the phone, and started to walk out of the store. The pharmacist turned to him and said, "Don't worry, son. You'll find a job as a gardener. Just keep looking."

The boy replied, "Oh, I'm not looking for work."

"But I thought I heard you asking for a job as a gardener," said the pharmacist.

The little boy dropped his gaze. Twisting a button on his jacket, he said, "Well, I am the gardener. I was just checking up on myself."

This little boy offers a good example of how important it is to conduct a check-up. An annual medical checkup is a must for good health. An auto tune-up on a regular basis is critical if you want to make sure everything is running well.

What about the maintenance needed to keep your life running smoothly? When was the last time you conducted an "attitude check-up" on yourself? Ask yourself, "What kind of job am I doing at work? How have I been treating others? What goals have I set for myself lately, and how am I going to reach them?"

Checkups are fairly simple to conduct. For the little boy, it was as easy as picking up the phone. By calling a time-out in your life and sitting down with yourself, you can gain much insight—and it won't even cost you a quarter.

One of the things that makes America the Land of Opportunity is that it's built on the concept of individual rights and achievement. When a society gives individuals the freedom to control their own destiny, people prosper. In contrast, the society that values group rights over individual rights flounders and decays.

The experiences of the early Pilgrims show how this principle works. When the Pilgrims landed at Plymouth Rock, they followed a socialistic economic plan. Everyone worked together. When the harvest was in, they shared their goods according to each person's need—and the Pilgrims almost starved to death.

Then a fortunate thing happened. The Pilgrims' new governor instituted a plan based on the principles of free enterprise. The governor said, "You will give 10 percent of all the goods you produce to the government to administer as needs arise. You can keep the remaining 90 percent." Right away productivity doubled. The following year it tripled, and America was on its way to becoming a great economic power.

The Pilgrims offer us a good lesson in economics. In order for free enterprise to be effective, productivity needs to be rewarded. When good work is rewarded, people become more productive and the society prospers. Conversely, when a society subsidizes losers and penalizes winners, that society will soon have more losers than winners.

Who are the people in your life who deserve to be rewarded for their labor? Maybe it's a colleague at work, a relative, or a friend. What would happen to their productivity if you rewarded them with a verbal pat on the back or a tangible expression of your appreciation? How would you feel if someone came up to you and said, "Hey, you really did a great job! I appreciate you, both for what you do and for who you are."

When you reward someone—financially or otherwise—for work well done, you help them experience the benefits of the free enterprise system. When people are richly rewarded for positive behavior, they will perform in a more positive way. It's the American way!

How to Act on Your Ideas

The world is filled with people who say, "I've got a great idea!" A lot of "great ideas," though, never get off the ground because the people behind them don't act on their intentions.

Two people who have acted on a great idea are Bill and Julie Price. As students at Southern Methodist University, they had an idea. They would sell a soft frozen dessert that tastes like ice cream but has half the calories, 80 percent less fat, and 30 percent more protein. Their dream became a reality when they bought two retail shops and opened for business under the name "I Can't Believe It's Yogurt."

People gobbled up Bill and Julie's idea. Customers choose from shakes, fruit smoothies, parfaits, and sundaes with 19 different toppings. As of July 1984, this brother-sister business team had opened 24 stores in Texas, Louisiana, Oklahoma, Tennessee, and New Mexico. And they plan to expand until folks in every part of the country are sampling their soft dessert and proclaiming, "I can't believe it's yogurt."

Bill and Julie didn't just think about their idea—they acted on it. They turned their dream into reality because they had the courage to take action.

Successful people know that the only rewarding idea is one that's acted on. How do you think fresh strawberry yogurt would taste if it were only an idea in your head?

If you really want to learn something and make it stick, then find out how to make it work. If you want to know how something tastes, don't just read the recipe—make it! If you want to know how Handel's *Messiah* sounds, why be content to hear the critics rave? Why not go to a live performance or, better yet, sing "The Hallelujah Chorus" yourself? Then you'll be acting on your idea!

How to Find a Need and Fill It

"Everyone is talking about the weather, but I don't see anyone doing anything about it," observed Mark Twain. And he had a point. Twain recognized the opportunities that await you once you determine a person's need and meet it.

One of people's greatest needs today is to know what the weather is going to do. And 60 businesses in the U.S. are meeting that need by forecasting weather conditions. The oldest and most successful of these is the Weather Services Corporation in Bedford, Massachusetts.

If you were to walk into their offices, you'd find an array of sophisticated computers and monitoring equipment gathering atmospheric data from around the globe. Information is beamed to television stations and compiled for *USA Today*'s bright, full-color weather map. In all, 600 clients rely on Weather Services Corporation because this firm is able to fill a need that's truly universal.

The firm has capitalized on an idea that's as old as the weather: If you want to be of value to others, find their need and seek to fill it. When you're motivated to give rather than to get, people will welcome you with open arms. They'll recognize your good intentions and tell you their dilemmas and their dreams.

When you help others fill a need, you give them a trusted friend and a winning solution. Serve others and I predict you'll experience a new warm climate of friendship in the days ahead.

Whatever happened to the old country store down on the corner? Where is the lovable owner who thought his business would last forever? Well, he and the store got leveled by the carry-out supermarket, the 10-acre K Mart, and the indoor mall. How can a lone businessman survive in the shadow of today's major department store chains which do more business in one day than a single proprietor does in an entire year?

If you've ever felt like David in a land of business Goliaths, take heart. There is a way you cannot only survive, but thrive as well. Some call it "going underground." I call it "fleeing to victory." When the opposition seems too huge, don't run from the giant—run between his legs. Darlene and Alan Resnick did this and found that the giant was too tall to bend over and catch them.

Darlene and Alan have become part of the recent pushcart phenomenon. This Boston couple found it impossible to start a major retail store. Darlene wanted to make and sell earmuffs, so she turned her kitchen table into a home factory. She started selling her wares from a pushcart in one of the city's big malls. Today her company has 800 wholesale accounts, some in major department stores. Darlene not only beat out the giants, but she won several over to her side.

Many small-business people today have found that the best

way to compete with large companies is to get smaller, not bigger. Ten years ago, you hardly ever saw a pushcart in a shopping center. Now you see them throughout the country in malls and parks, on street corners and sidewalks. With a pushcart, an individual can get into business on a shoestring.

You don't have to be in business to flee to victory. Your gigantic opponent might be a rocky relationship, a tough course in school, or a personal goal that seems impossible to reach. Whatever the situation, whatever the risk, you can do one of three things. You can either ignore the giant and run away; you can try to avoid Goliath and run around the problem; or you can face the giant head on.

It takes courage to dash between the legs of a giant. When you get to the point where you're willing to make your break, remember to run like crazy! You don't want to get stepped on!

How to Really Clean Up

If you were managing a team of discouraged employees, what's the most effective thing you could do to boost their morale?

As a manager, I would follow a worker who had just made a big mess. I would clean up after his mistake until he looked like a hero. And I can assure you it wouldn't be long before you'd see my employee's morale shoot up.

Let's face it. Sooner or later, you're going to have to deal with another person's mistake. The question is whether you are willing to make the most of it.

Did you know that some people make a living cleaning up after other people's messes? A growing number of professional housecleaning franchises earned $28.9 million in 1983 alone. A typical maid service grosses between $100,000 and $200,000 a year with profits of 19 to 28 percent. In a healthy economy, you might say that a maid really cleans up.

Your home may not need the dust rag of a full-time house cleaner. There are, however, at least two things you can learn from watching a pro mop up. First, a successful cleaning service knows how to make a house sparkle in a short amount of time. They've discovered a system that makes the best use of every possible minute. What would be the best use of your time in addressing a problem?

Second, successful house cleaners always work as a team.

Their motto is "divide the dirt and conquer." Who can you get to help clean up the mess that needs attention? Your work will go much more easily if someone pitches in. And even though the task may not be much fun, it will be a lot easier to share the load instead of toiling alone.

Housecleaning services have taught me something else, too. The world is not short on work. If you're looking for something to do, you don't have to go far. I wouldn't exactly look forward to picking up the pieces of my employee's error, but I would do it.

Believe it or not, some of my most satisfying work has involved cleaning up "disasters" in business. Come to think of it, I could have hired a maid service to do the work! But then I wouldn't have had the fun of getting my hands dirty or the satisfaction of seeing the smiles when my team pitched in and learned what it meant to really clean up.

How to Become a Billionaire

Wealth. Some people earn it. Others rob to get it. And still others—like J. Paul Getty—are born into it. Getty's father was an attorney who made a fortune drilling for oil. When he was ten, J. Paul Getty entered the oil business and he never left it. He died one of the world's richest men.

Someone once asked Getty, "How does a person become a billionaire?" He answered the question in two words: "Try harder." Although this phrase is much used, its wisdom doesn't seem to fade.

I remember asking a basketball coach about one of his players. "How good is he?," I wanted to know. The coach quickly replied, "He could be fantastic if he would just try harder."

Extra effort is needed everywhere, especially in business. Often I hear frustrated managers rave about their employees: "They could get promoted. They could be a great success. If they would just try harder!"

Floyd Fike is a perfect example of what it means to try hard. Floyd was born with a physical handicap that affects the tendons in his joints, and this makes basic things like walking and writing very difficult. Yet for the past several years, Floyd has worked many extra hours, walked many extra miles, and unselfishly given himself to others. Maybe that's why today he owns two successful real estate offices.

Floyd Fike had a choice: he could let his handicap limit him to mediocrity or motivate him to great achievements. Floyd accepted his physical condition and shifted his determination into high gear.

Floyd Fike decided to try harder. There was no magic involved. He simply said to himself, "I'm giving this job the extra effort it demands."

Somewhere right now there's a job, a relationship, a cause that's asking you to try harder. Reach beyond your limit. Try a little harder not because your extra effort might earn you a reward. Try harder for the best reason of all—because your work deserves it. You may not become a billionaire, but you'll become rich in ways that money can't buy.

John Ralston, a former college and professional football coach, once told me, "One of the best habits I've ever developed in my life is that of saving money."

Saving money has become a lost art in our credit-card culture. Most people, however, who reach their life goal do so because of resources that come from saving. If you want to achieve financial security, more freedom at work, and peace of mind, then you need to save regularly. The benefits are invaluable.

First, a savings plan can help provide the finances you need to live tomorrow. How much should you set aside from each paycheck? If you save just 10 percent of each paycheck and allow that money to grow and multiply, there will come a day when the income from your savings will exceed the income from your work.

Second, by saving regularly, you can find new freedom in your work. With a savings account to draw on, you can afford to wait out times of unemployment and seek the best possible job opportunity. You can avoid feeling the financial pressure of needing to jump at the first job that comes along. This means you can also work out of love for your job, rather than working because of financial necessity.

Third, a regular savings plan allows you to meet future needs (college education for your children, a new home, a secure retirement fund). The only way you can meet these and other high-ticket needs is with money you save.

Fourth, a savings plan will help you enjoy life more. For instance, I'm writing this while lounging on a sunny Mexican beach. I'm able to enjoy this vacation only because I built a savings plan through the years. The resort is filled with people who have learned the joy of setting aside a little today so they can enjoy themselves a little more tomorrow. They have saved and invested their money instead of consuming all of their earnings.

Finally, the more you save, the more you'll be able to experience the joy of giving. It's difficult to give from an empty purse. The more you save, the greater your capacity to help others.

It doesn't matter how much or how little you choose to set aside initially. You can start with a small savings account. What does matter is that by adding to your account regularly, you'll be motivated to save more.

By saving regularly and wisely, your earnings can literally last a lifetime.

P·A·R·T
THREE

PEOPLE

of Everyday Living

Jerry Caven was a young man when he began to teach school. He was also the father of five children. One of his biggest challenges was stretching his meager salary to clothe and feed his family.

During his search for solutions, Jerry learned that the local McDonald's hamburger stand in Boise, Idaho, had gone broke. He convinced the McDonald's people to sell him the franchise for the cost of the inventory. Jerry borrowed money on his house and within a few days went into the hamburger business.

In the first month, he took the Boise McDonald's from certain debt to surprising profit. During the next several years, Jerry built six equally successful McDonald's restaurants. Later he created and managed The Royal Fork restaurant chain that eventually spread throughout the western United States.

Jerry Caven took a risk because he wanted to reach his full potential. His story illustrates the principle that to be a success in life, you need more than just an opportunity. Nearly everyone will find an opportunity, but few are willing to act on the opportunity that's right before them.

Each of the people you'll read about in this third section has learned to live to his or her potential because each chose to act. Each turned everyday challenges into extraordinary feats.

Each of the people you'll meet is a living example of the principles and practical suggestions you've been reading about. You'll meet an unknown track coach who, with a desire to put others first, helped a lanky youth get to the Olympic Games. You'll meet a man who, despite having only one leg, literally stood up to a challenge few thought he could endure. And you'll meet a frightened college youth who found that he didn't have to be afraid when he "lost" his life to God.

Most of the people whom you'll meet in this section are still living out their stories. The books of their lives are still being written. So is yours. Your journey is not yet complete, and the road of life may turn in different and exciting new directions.

Somewhere in the next few pages, you may meet a person who will come alongside you and walk with you down that new road. When that happens, you'll see that their story is *your* story and that your shared journey can lead to the common destination of fulfillment.

John Johnson:
From the Bottom Up

America is known as the Land of Opportunity, and few people know that better than John Johnson.

John was born in Arkansas to parents who were dirt poor. They lived together in a small farmhouse that had no indoor toilet and no running water.

When John was six, his father died. John's mother had to work as a housekeeper and cook so that the two could survive. Later, John and his mother moved to Chicago where she found little work. The two lived mainly on welfare.

Despite his background, John was determined to make something of himself. He worked hard in school and distinguished himself as an outstanding student. He became president of his class and editor of the school newspaper and yearbook.

After graduating from high school, John went to college part-time and held down a full-time job with the Supreme Life Insurance Company. His diligence earned him a string of promotions: he advanced from office boy to assistant editor of the company newsletter and later to editor. Then John seized an opportunity that would change his life.

While reading *Reader's Digest* one day, John decided there should be a similar magazine for blacks. On $500 of borrowed money, he published a magazine called *Negro Digest*. He didn't stop there. In time, John became publisher of *Ebony* and several other leading magazines.

Though born and raised in poverty, John Johnson didn't become defeated. He didn't let circumstances dictate his life. Though he started at the bottom rung of society, he climbed as high as his dreams would take him.

Think of your current circumstances. Do they seem too cloudy, too confused? Then think of the boy who discovered the fact that America is a land where personal dreams *can* come true.

Joanne Wallace: A Growing Self-Image

"I really want to grow." I constantly hear people say this. They're bank executives, homemakers, teachers, pastors, and parents. They're people who want to grow—emotionally, spiritually, and financially; in their marriages, their churches, their careers.

So often, however, these same folks feel defeated because they suffer from a poor self-image. They should hear the story of Joanne Wallace.

When she was in her early twenties, Joanne worked in Salem, Oregon, on a frozen foods assembly line. She befriended a woman who was struggling with a poor self-image and tried to help her feel good about herself.

When Joanne heard about a self-improvement course, she suggested that her friend take the class. The woman said she'd be happy to enroll if Joanne would join her. Joanne agreed. As a result of the class, Joanne's friend grew in ways she never thought possible. Over the years, she's blossomed into a very successful woman.

And Joanne? She graduated at the top of her class, and she was asked to teach courses at the school. Eventually, Joanne became branch manager of the modeling agency.

Joanne didn't stop there. She started her own company. Today Joanne Wallace has trained over 1,000 instructors who teach self-improvement courses for women throughout the

United States and Canada. She has written two best-selling books on self-improvement and is a much sought-after speaker throughout the U.S. and Canada.

Joanne Wallace became a changed person because she reached out to someone in need. Had she kept to herself she might still be standing next to that same conveyor belt of frozen food. By investing a part of herself in someone else, Joanne grew far beyond her own little world. And the self-image of both women blossomed more than either of them could have imagined.

In life, you can look at others and wonder, "What's in it for me?," or you can care about others and ask, "What's in it for them?" Joanne Wallace's life is a testimony to the fact that people grow when they reach out to help others.

Somewhere in your neighborhood, your home, your work, or your school, there's someone who needs your help. Once you take that first step and reach out, you'll be able to look back and see how far you've moved away from serving yourself and towards serving others. And the distance between those two points is a measure of how far you've grown.

Sherman Kendall:
Down But Never Out

Have you ever felt like a failure? The next time you get knocked down and don't feel like getting back up, think of Sherman Kendall.

I met Sherman while giving a motivational speech at a hairdresser's convention. Sherman and his wife invited me to lunch where he told me how a painful failure changed his life.

Sherman had worked as a hairstylist for several years before he bought his own beauty salon. Initially he had a great time and thought his new venture would be very successful. Unfortunately, Sherman lacked business knowledge. He made some poor decisions and eventually went broke. "I became depressed and discouraged," he said. "I felt my life was ruined."

Sherman decided to analyze what had happened to him. He made a list of all the bad moves he had made with the salon. Then he wondered, "What would be the right way to handle these problems?"

Sherman wrote these thoughts down and published a book designed to help others avoid making the same mistakes. Sherman's book was such a hit that it's earned him more money than he lost with the salon.

In fact, the book opened a new career for Sherman. Today he's a speaker who shows others how to be successful in business. "I've even developed a nationwide line of beauty products," he adds, "that is now selling very, very well."

Sherman Kendall had a choice. He could either give up or get up. Instead of hiding his mistakes, he shared them with others. Sherman Kendall discovered that his dead end was actually a new beginning.

Do you see a dead end in your life? Take another look. Like Sherman, you just might be standing at a new beginning.

Willie Stokes:
What a Way to Go

Have you ever thought about someone who recently died and wondered, "What did he really value in life?" One way to find out is to look at that person's funeral. How a person chooses to be remembered when he dies says a lot about how he lived.

Take Willie Stokes, Jr. This Chicago man, shot to death when he was just 26, didn't want a traditional funeral or a traditional coffin. Willie's casket was designed to look like a Cadillac Seville. A local body-and-fender shop installed a fender and grille on the front. The casket had wheels and a license plate with the name "WIMP," Willie's nickname.

Dressed in a red velvet suit and fedora, Willie reclined in the front seat. On his fingers was a collection of diamond rings, and his hands were stuffed with wads of bills.

The picture of Willie Stokes is a haunting reminder that how you die will reflect how you lived. If your values and lifestyle were graphically portrayed by the way you were buried, what would your funeral look like? (I would like to be remembered like the alpine climber whose monument reads, "He died climbing.")

At his funeral, Willie Stokes showed the world what he valued. For you and me, death can affirm the way we choose to live. Death forces us to confess that what we believe is important for the here and now as well as the hereafter.

Too bad Willie Stokes is not around to hear this, but then his fate is already secure. (By the way, someone removed the rings and one hundred dollar bills from his coffin before he was buried.)

America is a nation living in fear. Today's magazines and medical journals are filled with stories of people who suffer from everything from acrophobia (fear of high places) to hydrophobia (fear of water). What things do you fear in life? If you find yourself afraid even to answer this question, then read the story of a young man who once lived in fear.

As a lad growing up, this man had a tremendous inferiority complex. He was terribly shy. When his family had guests over, he would hide in the attic or out in the woodshed. When his parents asked him to recite a poem, he was so afraid to stand up in front of people that he ran and hid.

The young man carried his fear of speaking into college. At Ohio Wesleyan, his phobia reached a peak. One day a teacher told him, "You're going to have to get on the ball, or you'll never amount to anything in life." As a result of that comment, the young man discovered his purpose in life—"to serve the Lord Jesus Christ and spread His Word as far as I possibly can in the course of my lifetime."

The young man who couldn't bring himself to face an audience was Norman Vincent Peale. His book *The Power of Positive Thinking* has been translated into 33 languages. Total publication has reached 18 million copies. Dr. Peale hosts a weekly television show, writes a syndicated weekly newspaper column, and is the co-editor of *Guideposts* magazine. Today, in his eighties, he still preaches every Sunday at the Marble Collegiate Church in New York City.

Do you sometimes feel like fear's prisoner? Is your life filled with phobias that seem too overwhelming to conquer? Then think of Norman Vincent Peale.

The next time you feel choked by fear's grip, think of a young boy hiding in an attic. Then picture him—confident, practiced, and poised—stepping before an audience of hundreds. The next time fear comes to visit, think of the man who gave himself to a needy world. His worst fear faded, and he grew into an effective and gifted public speaker. Proof positive that you can claim power over fear and that what appears to be a weakness may in reality be an untapped inner strength.

Charles Riley:
Berlin's Other Hero

Jesse Owens is a name familiar to all sports fans. Even those who don't follow track and field have seen pictures of this famous American athlete standing on the victor's stand at the 1936 Berlin Olympic Games. Jesse Owens embarrassed Adolf Hitler and thrilled a watching world by collecting four gold medals. He placed first in the 100- and 200-meter dashes, the 400-meter relay, and the broad jump.

The free world cheered for Jesse Owens. But the world would never have applauded Jesse Owens had it not been for Charles Riley.

Charles Riley was Jesse's junior high track coach. He took a special interest in the small, timid black boy from Alabama. Riley saw the athletic potential in Jesse and told him he could be a great runner—if he wanted to work at it.

Jesse believed his coach and proceeded to run into the record books. Years later this Olympic champion said that it was Charles Riley who gave him hope that he could be someone and do something exciting in his life. Thanks to the influence of Charles Riley, Jesse Owens realized that he had the potential for greatness.

Behind every Jesse Owens there's likely to be a Charles Riley, someone whose encouragement and faith say, "You *can* do it! You may not see your full potential, but I do."

Who is the Charles Riley in your life? What has he or she said and done to make you want to reach your full potential? Jesse Owens gave so much to the world because someone named Charles Riley, who never wore an Olympic medal, gave so much to him.

It's both humbling and thrilling to think that you can become a Charles Riley for someone else. Right now, someone in your life is waiting for you to pass the torch. Who is waiting to receive what you have to give?

Carl Joseph:
Standing Tall

As a high school athlete, Carl Joseph enjoyed the kind of success that made headlines and won him praise. In three years, this young man from Madison, Georgia, earned 14 letters in three sports.

As a starting defensive lineman, he was one of his football team's most effective rushers. On the basketball court, Carl scored points with his patented slam dunk. In track he excelled in the high jump.

Carl's achievements were no more remarkable than those of his teammates—except for one thing. Carl Joseph has only one leg.

Imagine sacking quarterbacks, busting through a line to block punts, and grounding opposing running backs with one leg. Imagine covering the length of a basketball court, passing, dribbling, and scoring—all this with only one leg. Imagine clearing 5'10" in the high jump with just half the vertical leaping capacity of your competition.

His physical handicap did not sideline Carl Joseph. When he was just sixteen months old, Carl learned to hop around his house. He could have resigned himself to a chair or to the slow, awkward stride of an artificial limb.

But Carl Joseph wouldn't let his disability limit how fast or how far he could go in life. Instead of moping, he got up and moved. A physical handicap didn't bench Carl Joseph. It motivated him to beat his circumstances.

After graduating from high school, Carl attended the University of Pittsburgh on a football scholarship. Because he was missing a limb, the NCAA prohibited Carl's participation on the field, so he managed the Panthers from the sidelines.

Today, this former athlete wants to become a trainer for a team in the National Football League. If you doubt he'll make it, just picture an 18-year-old pouring in points for his high-school basketball team or squirming through an offensive line.

When I think of Carl Joseph, I don't see a disability. I see a courageous individual who won't let his circumstances defeat his will to succeed.

Whenever you feel limited by circumstances, think of Carl Joseph. Suddenly your own handicaps may not seem so overwhelming. The only thing holding you back may be your hesitation to answer the question, "How high do I want to go?"

Tom Landry: Always in Control

Tom Landry knows what it means to be a winner. And he should. He coached the Dallas Cowboys to Super Bowl victories in 1972 and 1978. In 1985, after completing his 26th year as the team's only field general, Tom Landry had compiled a career win-loss record of 166-67. That's a 71 percent winning record, second-best on the all-time list of pro football coaches.

Years before he ever walked the sidelines, Tom Landry learned the secret of being in control. During World War II, when he was only 19, his B-17 Bomber crash-landed. Landry brought the plane down between two trees which sheared off his craft's wings. He and the rest of the crew walked away without a scratch.

Tom Landry learned how to be in control in the locker room as well. As a 24-year-old defensive back for the New York Giants, he listened as his coach tried to explain a new defensive plan designed to help them beat the Cleveland Browns. After the coach left the room, the players stared at each other with a look of "Now what do we do?"

Landry took control. He walked to the blackboard and began to explain to his teammates what they had to do to make their coach's plans work. Landry communicated, the team won, and a new coach was born. In 1960, Tom Landry was given the chance to coach a new team, the Dallas Cowboys.

The average life span of most NFL coaches is four years. Tom Landry held the same post six times as long—for nearly a quarter of a century! How did he endure? He might tell you that, on the field of battle, football, or life, the secret of being in control is to let God take control of your life.

Tom Landry would say you don't get control by holding onto the reins, but by letting go; not by dominating others, but by serving them. The former coach of the Dallas Cowboys maintains that his purpose in life is to serve God in whatever way He requires. This faith, says Landry, gives him strength and an inner peace that touches every area of life. And for him, the secret is yielding to the One who's always in control.

Larry Bird:
Total Effort, True Reward

In 1973, he was an unknown 16-year-old from French Lick, Indiana, who couldn't even make his high-school basketball team. Yet, ten years later, Larry Bird was one of the greatest players in the history of professional basketball. How did he do it?

Larry Bird was one of the most unlikely candidates for greatness. Coaches and friends thought he was too slow and too small to play basketball. It wasn't until he grew four inches between his junior and senior years in high school that Larry Bird began to attract the attention of college scouts.

Personal adversity was another opponent for Larry. After he graduated from high school, Larry's parents divorced and his father committed suicide. Larry Bird didn't know where to light. He went to three different colleges before settling in at Indiana State. After sitting out his entire freshman year, Larry came into his own on the basketball court. In 1979, Larry Bird led his team to a second-place finish in the NCAA championships.

What would you do if it looked like you were too short to reach your goal? How would you react if your family suddenly split apart? What would you think if you were asked to sit on the bench?

By confronting and hurdling some of life's toughest obstacles, Larry Bird has developed a tenacity and toughness that translate into greatness on the basketball court. You can see it every time he plays because Larry Bird gives 100 percent of himself.

Total effort. It's essential if you want to reach your goal in life. Giving your total effort can help you overcome physical limitations. It can help you deal with personal tragedy.

By giving his all, Larry Bird has earned a reputation as one of the greatest NBA players of all time. On the basketball court, Larry Bird has found his reward for total dedication. Where will you experience the rewards of giving your all?

John Zehr:
Opportunity in Simple Things

One of my favorite things to do as a boy was walk on the bank of the Snake River in the Pacific Northwest. I would bend down, find the flattest stone I could, and then see how many times I could make it skip across the water. Sometimes they nose-dived with one plop, but other times my stones bounced off the lake and kept rising as if under their own power. It was magic and I loved it.

John Zehr is a man who shares my love for skipping stones. When he wound up and threw, however, John saw more than just flat rocks dancing on the water. He saw a way to share his experience with others.

"Could there possibly be a market for skipping stones?" he wondered. Yes, there could. After experimenting with more than 30 designs in hard plaster, John came up with what he called "the stone with the dimple." The dimple, he says, holds air beneath the stone so that it jumps off the water more often, causing it to skip longer.

John took his creation to market. Today, his Orbiter World-Class Skipping Stones have landed in numerous novelty shops. Sales of the stones (which come 20 to a tube) even skipped all the way to Europe where a Paris advertising agency bought 150 tubes.

John Zehr is not going to change the course of world history with his invention. He did, however, do something unassuming yet profound. He took an everyday boyhood pastime and passed his pleasure on to someone else. In bending down to pick up a simple rock, he found a way to make someone happy. What made his discovery so special, I believe, is that it came out of an everyday situation.

A guy like John Zehr makes me realize that the movers and shakers of the world aren't necessarily the ones with the high-octane lifestyles and high-powered careers. In fact, the people who often make the greatest contributions are the everyday folk whose uncommon genius springs from life's most common pleasures.

It's been a long time since I walked down by the Snake River and skipped stones. But, like the banks of the Snake River, life is filled with thousands of opportunities. Which ones will you choose to pick up and share with someone else?

Ruth and Ben Emery:
Licking the Competition

I recently ordered a set of cassettes from a well-known speaker. Unfortunately, my eagerness to hear his message soon turned sour. This man had recorded the same speech at six different meetings with six different titles and then sold the one address as a "sales training package."

This "respected expert" was more concerned about fattening his income than satisfying his customers. He had put profit ahead of people. I didn't fully understand the significance of his choice until I learned about Ben and Ruth Emery, operators of the KR Drive-In in Rice Hills, Oregon.

When Ben and Ruth opened their restaurant in 1970, they made a commitment to give their customers real value for their money. And it all started with ice cream.

Today, Ben and Ruth feature ice cream cones that weigh $6\frac{1}{2}$ ounces for $.50. That's three times the amount of ice cream at nearly half the price of most other stores. The Emerys also sell a giant 16-ounce version of their confection for $1.25. (Shovel not included.)

In between licks, customers may wonder, "This is such a great deal. How can these folks ever be successful?" The answer is evident in their ice cream delivery orders—the Emerys sell a lot of ice cream! In 1972, after only two months in business, they sold over 37,000 gallons of ice cream—the highest volume sold by a drive-in or restaurant in Oregon that year.

Ice cream isn't the only value the Emerys dish up. Their hamburgers, French fries, and other menu items are priced just as reasonably. The result is that the KR Drive-In has attracted customers from throughout the Northwest and around the world.

Unfortunately, many people think there's a rule of business that says, "Quality or quantity—choose one or the other." Ben and Ruth Emery have broken that rule by giving people quality *and* quantity.

The Emerys have proven that when you serve people an honest deal, they come back for more. In an age of shrinking ice cream cones and rising prices, the KR Drive-In is an uncommon reminder that you don't have to reduce the size of your product, jack up the price, or compromise your service to be successful. For the Emerys, success means putting the customer first.

Whether you're at work, school, or home, you can serve others with quantity *and* quality. And you'll never have to worry about a lack of customers.

The Excalibre Team:
At the Edge of Adventure

Being successful and being young. The two don't always go together. If you're just starting out in your career, you'll probably have to be content to learn, grow, and wait your turn—unless you happen to be one of the four executives who founded the Excalibre Software Company of Seattle, Washington.

While a number of competitors might easily surpass Excalibre's sales goal of $1 million, they probably don't come close to the ages of Excalibre's founding members: David Galespie, 18; Steven Trenan, 17; Richard Clark, 15; and John Stam, 15.

When these four started out, older and wiser "experts" may have told them things like, "You're simply too young to be doing what you're doing," "You need more experience," or "Try out your idea in a few years after you've grown up. Then you might make it."

Energy and youth have given this team of entrepreneurs an edge over the competition. Today, Excalibre products are drawing rave reviews from as far away as West Germany and Saudi Arabia. The firm is now on the verge of landing contracts with major American companies like Chrysler Corporation. And the Excalibre wizards hope to grow even further with action games like "Moon Blaster." In the often up-and-down computer market, Excalibre is rocketing forward on the power of youthful zeal and good ideas.

Excalibre's founders discovered their potential as business innovators and leaders when they chose to risk. They weren't content to obey the counselors of extreme caution whose "wisdom" said, "Don't try anything daring until you have a proven track record."

David, Steven, Richard, and John didn't wait until they were 40 to get out of the blocks. When others were still warming up, they ran ahead and discovered you're never too young to start.

Ron Schaffsma:
Going the Extra Mile

Somewhere between his boyhood home of Artesia, California, and his current business, Ron Schaffsma took an old axiom to heart and learned to "go the extra mile." By giving of himself generously, he has become the president of Country Stoves, one of the most successful wood stove manufacturing companies in the Pacific Northwest.

Most people want instant success, but Ron Schaffsma learned that true reward comes from going the extra mile through the years. While he was a young man, for instance, Ron learned the value of saving. Instead of blowing his money, he saved his allowance. Years later, Ron was able to cash in on rewarding business opportunities because he had the needed dollars at hand.

Ron also went the extra mile at work. He didn't punch out at 5:00 p.m. He committed himself to giving his boss more than a full day's work for a full day's pay. Ron's attitude didn't say, "Pay me more and I'll work more," but rather, "I'll work and get the job done because it's the right thing to do."

When Ron was in charge, his employees saw their boss' extra miles add up. Ron tackled jobs his peers were unwilling to do. He picked up after others. He didn't avoid weeds; he pulled them. If a screw was loose, he tightened it. If one of his employees was hurt, Ron was at his side to help.

When you consistently go the extra mile as Ron does, you can't help but move further away from a self-centered existence and closer to the satisfaction of helping others. Going the extra mile may make your journey lonely and long. If, however, your heart is in the right place, then people can't help but see the joy you have in serving others. They'll see that going the extra mile is worth the extra effort, and they'll want to join you. That's when people stop doing only the minimum and start discovering the maximum reward of looking beyond themselves.

CONCLUSION

I believe that you do one of two things with every book you read. You either put it back on the shelf and eventually forget what the author said. Or you carry that book with you and allow its message to carve out a very real place in your life.

I hope by now the principles, strategies, and people you've read about in this book have become so real to you that you will never forget them. As you think about Ed Foreman's "Ten Commandments for Happiness and Success," Carl Joseph who hopped to success on one leg, or the paperboy who said, "I'm sorry," I hope you carry with you the following three thoughts:

1. *Love the person you see in the mirror. You won't find another one quite like him/her.*
    Translation: God made you a unique person. Your talents, your personality, your ambitions will never be duplicated in anyone else. You will do things in your lifetime that no one else will ever accomplish. No one can help women blossom to their full potential quite like Joanne Wallace does. No one can work with a basketball quite like Larry Bird.
    Discover and develop your uniqueness as a person, and you will begin to find new direction and meaning in life.

2. *If you really love it, let it go.*

Translation: The only way you can truly enjoy your life is to give it away to others. Your time, your ideas, your money—to the degree you invest these in other people, you'll experience an inner satisfaction that truly goes beyond words.

I've seen this paradox come to life in each of the people mentioned in this book. Your unique contribution can only be realized when others receive what you have to give them. Loosen your grip on your ambitions, your resources, your dreams. Share them with others, and life will take on new meaning as you see your life being used for good.

3. *Do it now, for the chance may be gone tomorrow.*

Translation: The only ideas that have real value are those that are acted on. To fulfill your dreams, you need to act on them. Action is starting the business you've long dreamed of owning. Action is building the home you've always wanted. Putting your goals into action means spending that long-delayed free evening with your family.

Would you rather be satisfied with daydreams or fulfilled by a life of action? Think about the common, everyday folks in these pages who accomplished uncommon feats by acting on their deepest aspirations. Is the choice easier now?

Let me leave you with one final thought. None of the stories in this book has really come to an end. They are still being lived out by the people who have been touched by the Joanne Wallaces and the Charles Rileys of this world. The story of a Tom Landry or a Ron Schaffsma can become your story as you make their vision your own.

Take the ideas, the people, the lessons of these pages to heart. May others see in you something that is so unique and beautiful that they will want to discover their own God-given qualities and live life to the fullest.

May you wake up in the morning with new enthusiasm and a new curiosity for all that the new day holds. May the words and ideas of this book, still fresh in your mind, plant the seeds of some surprising and new possibilities for growth in the opportunities of everyday life that are waiting for you right now!